Table of Contents

Executive Summary

When consumers purchase their credit scores from one of the major nationwide consumer reporting agencies (CRAs), they often receive scores that are not generated by the scoring models use to generate scores sold to lenders. The Dodd-Frank Wall Street Reform and Consumer Protection Act directed the Consumer Financial Protection Bureau (CFPB) to compare credit scores sold to creditors and those sold to consumers by nationwide CRAs and determine whether differences between those scores disadvantage consumers. CFPB analyzed credit scores from 200,000 credit files from each of the three major nationwide CRAs: TransUnion, Equifax, and Experian. The study yielded the following results:

- The CFPB found that for a majority of consumers the scores produced by different scoring models provided similar information about the relative creditworthiness of the consumers. That is, if a consumer had a good score from one scoring model the consumer likely had a good score on another model. For a substantial minority, however, different scoring models gave meaningfully different results.

- Correlations across the results of scoring models were high, generally over .90 (out of a possible one). Correlations were stronger among the models for consumers with scores below the median than for consumers with scores above the median.

- To determine if score variations would lead to meaningful differences between the consumers' and lenders' assessment of credit quality, the study divided scores into four credit-quality categories. The study found that different scoring models would place consumers in the same credit-quality category 73-80% of the time. Different scoring models would place consumers in credit-quality categories that are off by one category 19-24% of the time. And from 1% to 3% of consumers would be placed in categories that were two or more categories apart.

- The study looked at results within several demographic subgroups. Different scores did not appear to treat different groups of consumers systematically differently than other scoring models. The study found less variation among scores for younger consumers and consumers who live in lower-income or high-minority population ZIP codes than for older consumers or consumers in higher-income or lower-minority population ZIP codes. This is likely driven by differences in the median scores of these different categories of consumers.

- Consumers cannot know ahead of time whether the scores they purchase will closely track or vary moderately or significantly from a score sold to creditors. Thus, consumers should not rely on credit scores they purchase exclusively as a guide to how creditors will view their credit quality.

- Firms that sell scores to consumers should make consumers aware that the scores consumers purchase could vary, sometimes substantially, from the scores used by creditors.

1. Introduction

Section 1078 of the Dodd-Frank Wall Street Reform and Consumer Protection Act directs the Consumer Financial Protection Bureau (CFPB) to conduct a study on the *"nature, range, and size of variations between the credit scores sold to creditors and those sold to consumers by consumer reporting agencies that compile and maintain files on consumers on a nationwide basis … and whether such variations disadvantage consumers."*[1]

On July 19, 2011, the CFPB published a report on *"The impact of differences between consumer- and creditor-purchased credit scores."* That report provided a description of the credit scoring industry; of the types of credit scores that are sold to consumers and businesses; and of the potential problems for consumers of having discrepancies between the scores they purchase and the scores used for decision-making by lenders in the marketplace.

That report also outlined a data analysis to be undertaken by the CFPB to describe credit score variations on approximately 200,000 credit files from three nationwide consumer reporting agencies (CRAs) – TransUnion, Equifax, and Experian – using credit scores typically sold to consumers and to creditors. This second report presents the findings of this analysis.

1.1 Overview of score variations and why they might matter

As described in the July 2011 CFPB study, when a consumer purchases a score from a nationwide CRA, it is likely that the credit score will not be the same as the score used by a particular lender or other commercial credit report user in making a lending or other score-based decision with respect to that consumer. The variation in scores reflects not only differences between scores sold to consumer and scores sold to creditors, but also differences among scores sold to creditors.

1.1.1 Types of Scores

Lenders use a wide variety of credit scores which vary by score provider, by model, and by target industry.

1.1.1.a FICO Scores

One consulting firm estimates that scores developed by Fair Isaac Corporation (FICO) accounted for over 90% of the market of scores sold to firms in 2010 for use in credit-related decisions.[2] There are numerous FICO scoring models that vary by version (e.g., newer and older models), by the nationwide CRA that sells the score to lenders, and by industry.

FICO's most current model is FICO 08, but commercial users still use earlier versions of FICO products. Additionally, FICO's generic scoring models – the most common FICO scores that are developed to predict performance on all types of credit - vary across the nationwide CRAs because the FICO scoring models are designed specifically for each CRA and reflect differences in how they organize and present credit report data.

FICO offers industry-specific models for credit cards, mortgages, auto loans, and telecommunication services. FICO models typically generate credit scores in the range between 300 and 850. FICO also builds custom models that are designed for specific companies' credit underwriting needs.

1.1.1.b Vantage Scores

VantageScore LLC, a score development company established as a joint venture of Equifax, TransUnion, and Experian, licenses its scoring models for sale by the three nationwide CRAs to both creditors and consumers. There are currently two Vantage scoring models in use: VantageScore and VantageScore 2.0. The original VantageScore® launched in 2006. VantageScore 2.0, developed using data from 2006 to 2009, launched in October 2010. The VantageScore models produce scores in the range of 501-990.

1.1.1.c Consumer Reporting Agency Scores

CRAs are companies that gather, organize, standardize, and disseminate consumer information, especially credit information. Each of the nationwide CRAs – Equifax, TransUnion, and Experian - have their own proprietary generic scoring models to predict credit performance. These models were originally developed for use by lenders to predict performance on credit obligations, but are now primarily sold as educational scores to consumers.[3] These scores typically resemble FICO scores in range. Some of the proprietary generic scores sold by the CRAs are:

- Equifax: "Equifax Credit Score." Produces scores in the range 280-850.[4]
- Experian: "Experian Plus Score." Produces scores in the range 330-830.[5]
- TransUnion: "TransRisk New Account Score." Produces scores in the range 300-850.[6]

In addition to being sold to consumers on a stand-alone basis, educational scores are often the scores provided by the CRAs to consumers who have purchased or otherwise subscribed to credit monitoring services, which typically provide reports and scores on a regular basis.

1.1.2 Consumer Purchases of Credit Scores

While consumers can obtain free annual credit reports from the nationwide CRAs, they typically have to pay for credit scores.[7] Consumers purchase scores through several channels. In most cases, the scores consumers purchase are educational credit scores made available to them by the nationwide CRAs and through other channels. Consumers may purchase scores by contacting a nationwide CRA directly or by purchasing a score to accompany the free credit reports consumers are able to obtain annually at annualcreditreport.com. The nationwide CRAs generally sell consumers educational scores or VantageScore scores. Consumers can also obtain credit scores by subscribing to credit monitoring services. Again, these scores are typically educational. Some educational credit scoring providers make scores available to consumers for free.

In some circumstances consumers can purchase FICO scores. For example, Equifax offers a FICO score for sale with an Equifax credit report, and consumers' FICO scores derived from credit reports from both Equifax and TransUnion can be purchased from FICO's consumer website, myfico.com. Consumers cannot purchase a FICO score generated from an Experian credit report. Even where a consumer purchases a FICO score and goes to a creditor that uses FICO scores, the score may not be the one any particular creditor uses, given the diversity of scores in the marketplace and the possibility that the creditor may obtain scores from a different CRA.

1.1.3 Potential Harms for Consumers

Variations between the credit scores sold to consumers and to lenders carry significance only if such variations lead to consumer harms. The July 19, 2011 CFPB Report highlighted potential harms for consumers. These harms include those resulting from consumers' inaccurate perceptions of their own credit worthiness.

1.1.3.a Harms from Inaccurate Perception of Creditworthiness

A consumer can face harms if, after purchasing a credit score, the consumer has a different impression of his or her creditworthiness than a lender would. If the score leads the consumer to overestimate lenders' likely assessment of his or her creditworthiness, the consumer might be likely to apply for credit lines that would not be approved, with a cost of wasted time and effort on both the consumer's and lender's part. Alternatively, the consumer may reject offers of credit that would be beneficial because the consumer's misperception of his or her creditworthiness leads the consumer to believe that the offers are over-priced.

If a consumer underestimates lenders' likely assessment of his or her creditworthiness, the consumer might fail to apply for credit at all or delay applying for credit, forgoing the opportunity to buy a house or car, for example, or delaying a valuable mortgage refinancing. A consumer might also apply to lenders who offer less favorable terms than he or she might qualify for, or accept less favorable offers received through the mail or online direct marketing. In this case, the cost to the affected consumer would be higher interest costs and possibly higher likelihoods of default due to the greater costs and difficulty of making monthly payments. Lenders might benefit by being able to charge higher interest to consumers who "incorrectly" understand their options when applying; at the same time lenders would lose out on business from consumers who decide not to apply for credit due to a misperception of its likely cost. Finally, consumers who believe their credit score to be low may take costly steps that they believe may improve their credit score.

1.1.3.b Small differences, Big impacts

Notably, the potential for a consumer to be confused may be greater where the consumer is sophisticated about the use of credit scores by creditors. Many lenders use specific score levels as thresholds to determine whether consumers will qualify for a particular loan or interest rate. For example, FICO score levels 620, 680, and 740 might be used by a lender as the boundary lines between consumers considered to be "sub-prime, "near-prime," or "prime" credit risks, respectively. A striking example of this is the fact that Fannie Mae generally won't buy mortgages with FICO scores under 620.[8] So, for consumers whose scores are in the relevant range, a small variation in a consumer's score might result in his or her score falling above or below such a cut-off, with dramatic implications for his or her access to home loans. Given the use of score thresholds to determine eligibility for certain products or pricing tiers, even small variations can have large impacts for certain consumers. If a consumer believes incorrectly that he falls above or below a crucial threshold then the impact of a given difference between scores may be magnified, since it may be more likely to have an impact on the consumer's perceptions and consequent credit-seeking behavior.

1.1.4 Study Objectives

To explore these issues, the CFPB undertook this follow-up study to the July 19, 2011 CFPB Report on credit scores to examine scores sold to consumers and see how well they correlate with the scores used by lenders.

2. Analysis and Results

This chapter of the report describes the data analyzed and presents results of several approaches to analyzing differences and similarities across scoring models.

The CFPB found that for a majority of consumers the scores produced by different scoring models provide similar information about the relative creditworthiness of the consumers. That is, if a consumer had a good score from one scoring model the consumer likely had a good score on another model. For a substantial minority, however, different scoring models gave meaningfully different results.

2.1 Data

Each of the three larger nationwide CRAs, Equifax, Experian, and TransUnion, provided the CFPB with a random sample of 200,000 consumer reports and credit scores calculated on such reports. The samples were chosen independently at the three CRAs; the samples were not designed to contain the same individuals. The samples selected included only reports with at least one trade line – and not, for example, simply an inquiry – that therefore would be potentially "scoreable" by at least one scoring model.

For each consumer report in the sample, the CRAs provided five credit scores; the file's trade line history, scrubbed of any potentially personally identifiable information; and ZIP code and age information to allow the CFPB to compare scores by consumer demographics.[9]

The five credit scores provided by each nationwide CRA for the study were:

1. The generic FICO[10] score sold by the CRA. Equifax provided BEACON 5, a FICO score; Experian provided FICO V2 (Quest); and TransUnion provided FICO Classic 2004.
2. The CRA's educational score sold to consumers. Equifax provided EquifaxRisk 3.0 scores, Experian provided Experian PLUS scores, and TransUnion provided TransRisk New Account Scores.
3. VantageScore 1.0.
4. FICO Auto Loan industry-specific score.
5. FICO BankCard industry-specific score.

The FICO scores and VantageScore are all sold to creditors. The generic FICO score (in some circumstances), the VantageScore, and the educational scores are sold to consumers. There are therefore a number of potential situations where the consumer could purchase a score and a creditor could purchase a different score to evaluate the creditworthiness of that consumer. The situations that can be evaluated with the data are: the consumer buys an educational score and the creditor uses a FICO score; the consumer buys an educational score and the creditor uses a VantageScore; the consumer buys a VantageScore and the creditor uses a FICO score; and, the consumer buys a FICO score and the creditor uses a VantageScore. Note that the last two situations are symmetric, and therefore there are three relevant pair-wise comparisons for each of the analyses: educational versus FICO, educational versus VantageScore, and VantageScore versus FICO. Analysis showed that the industry-specific scores are very highly correlated to the generic FICO scores, and therefore comparisons with those models are not presented – results were very similar to analysis of the generic FICO score.[11]

The results of the analysis were extremely similar qualitatively across the three CRAs. The study therefore presents results from a single CRA in the body of the report and provides results for the other two CRAs in the Appendix. There is one exception to this broader pattern. The sample provided by one of the CRAs contained very few young consumers because of the way the sample was drawn. Adjusting for this difference (e.g., focusing on older consumers) the results for this CRA are very similar to the other two CRAs.[12]

2.2 Analysis and Results

2.2.1 Score Distributions

In order to better understand differences in scores across models, and in anticipation of some of the results shown later in the report, it is useful to have some background on the distribution of scores across consumers.

In addition to the score range that score developers select, developers determine the shape of the distribution of scores. This is because scores rank consumers according to their relative risk and therefore the relationship between score and absolute risk does not have to be constant across the score range. Figure 1 shows the score distributions for the three models for one of the CRAs. It shows that the FICO score and the educational score are scaled such that there is a large proportion of scores in the higher end and a long "tail" at the lower end of the score distribution, while the VantageScore is scaled such that the distribution of scores is relatively flat across the score distribution. This means that small changes in a FICO score or educational score at the high end of the score distribution translate into relatively large percentile changes, while changes in score at the low end of the FICO or educational score range translate into relatively small percentile changes. For VantageScore, on the other hand, a given score change leads to a similar percentage change across the score distribution.

FIGURE 1: SCORE DISTRIBUTIONS

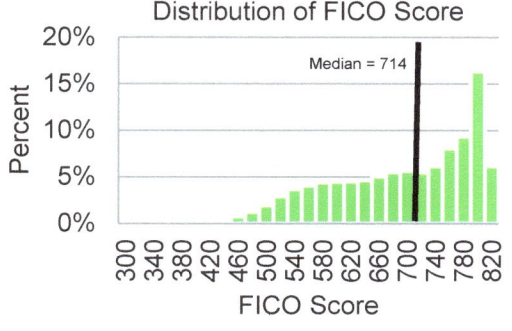

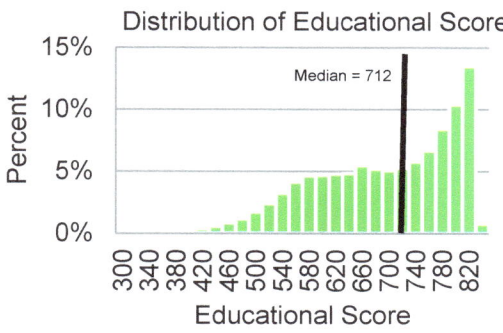

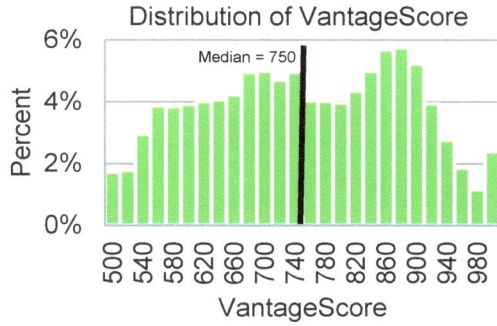

All credit scoring models rank individual consumers by their *relative* credit risk. That is, a score represents a consumer's likelihood of becoming delinquent on a loan *relative to the risk of other consumers who represent lower risks (i.e., have higher scores) or higher risk (i.e., have lower scores)*. For a given population and time period, however, absolute default probabilities can be calculated. Figure 2 shows an example of default risk by FICO score. It shows that at the low end of the score range the risk of default is very high and the relationship between score and risk is fairly steep, while at the high of the score distribution, where risk is very low, the relationship is fairly flat. This means that score differences at the low end of the score distribution are associated with relatively large differences in default probability, while score differences at the high end are associated with relatively small differences in default probability.

FIGURE 2: DEFAULT RISK BY FICO SCORE[13]

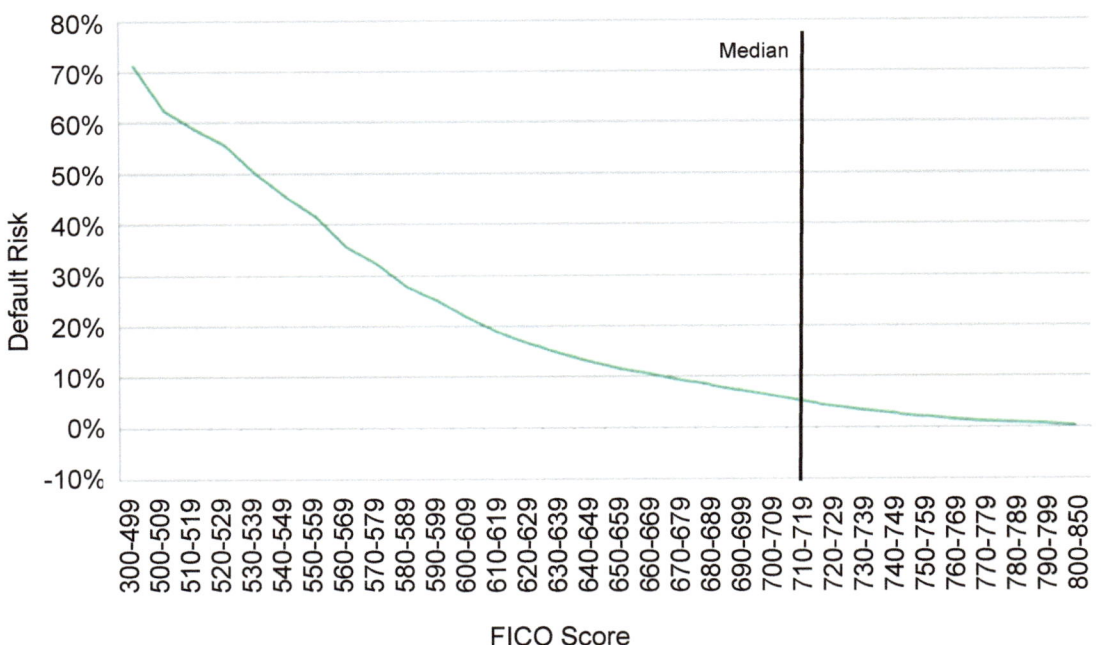

2.2.2 Adjusting for Score Range Differences

As discussed in the introduction, different scoring models use different ranges. FICO scores have a 300-850 range, educational scores resemble the FICO range with minor variations, and VantageScore ranges from 500-990. In order to make useful comparisons across scoring models the scores were first converted into a relative score. This was done separately for each scoring model. Consumers were first ranked by score. Their percentile in the distribution of scores was then determined, and this was the "relative score" used throughout the analysis. For example, consider a consumer with a FICO score of 680. The score places the consumer at the 38th percentile of the FICO score distribution, meaning he or she has a better FICO score than 38% of consumers. His or her relative score for the FICO model was therefore 38. This was also done for the VantageScore and the educational score. This allowed us to compare where consumers fell in the score distribution using each of the models, and disentangle these differences from the differences that arose because different scoring models use different score ranges. We use the phrase "relative score" to mean the percentile equivalent of the score generated by a particular model.

2.2.3 Correlation across Scoring Models

The simplest measure of similarity or difference of the scores produced by the different scoring models is "correlation." Correlation is a measure of how closely related two variables are, and ranges from -1 to 1. A value of -1 indicates that two variables have a perfectly inverse relationship, while a value of 1 means they are perfectly related. A value of zero means that there is no relationship between the two variables. So, the closer the correlation between the scores produced by two models is to 1, the tighter the relationship between those scoring models, and the more similar the two scores will be for a given consumer (on average).

Figure 3 provides visual representations of these relationships. It shows "scatter-plot" graphs that show consumers' relative scores from pairs of scoring models. A dot represents consumers with the given combination of scores (as shown on the axes); dot size shows the relative number of consumers that have a given combinations of scores. (The "lumpiness" in the figures arises from using percentiles; there were some score "ties" that lead to more than 1% of consumers being assigned the same score percentile.) These figures each showed clearly that there is a relationship between the scores produced by these models for each consumer, but scores were not perfectly correlated. Figure 3 also shows that there appeared to be greater dispersion between the pairs of scores above the median, so that scores were more similar for consumers with worse scores and less similar for consumers with better scores.

FIGURE 3: SCATTERPLOTS

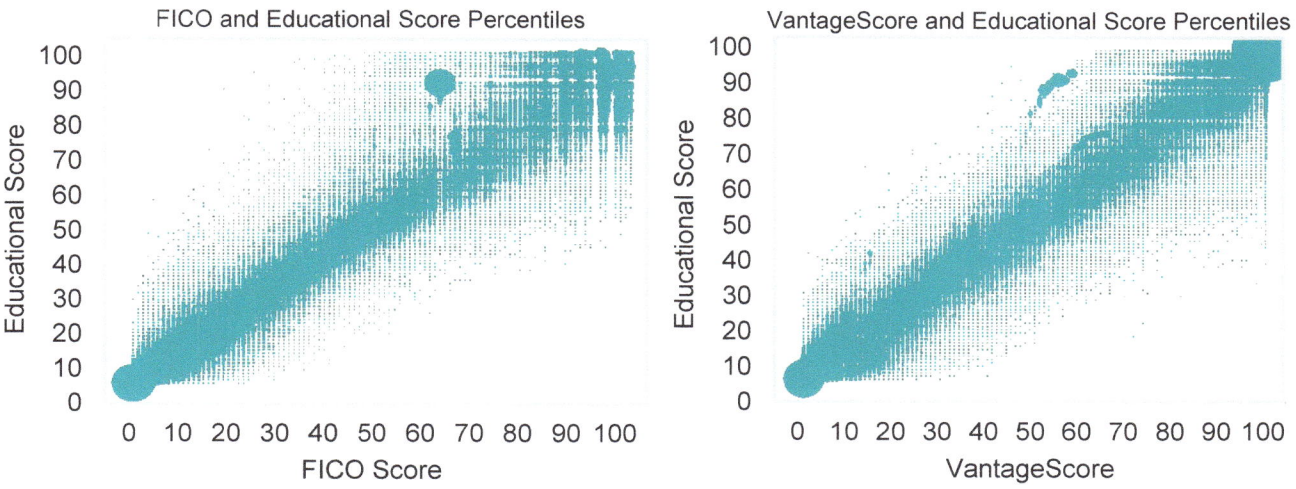

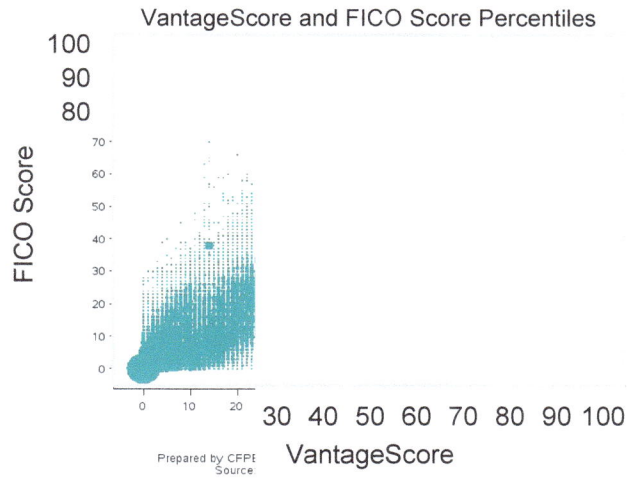

Figure 4 shows the correlations for each of the pairs of scoring models. It shows that the correlations were high, in each case equal to or greater than 0.9. Figure 4 also shows the correlations when the sample was split into low-score and high-score groups, using the average percentile across the two groups and splitting at the median (the 50th percentile). It confirms what is apparent from the figure, that scores, as measured by score percentile, were less closely correlated for high-score consumers than low-score consumers.

FIGURE 4: SCORE CORRELATIONS

	Overall	Customers Below Median		Customers Above Median
FICO vs. Educational	0.93	0.86	>	0.64
Vantage vs. Educational	0.93	0.82	>	0.68
Vantage vs. FICO	0.90	0.77	>	0.52

Figure 2 provides some insight into why scores were more highly correlated for low-score consumers than for high-score consumers. As shown in Figure 2, there was much less variation in default risk above the median (ranging from roughly 0% to 5%) than below (where it ranges from roughly 5% to over 60%). This is true for VantageScore as well, as shown in Appendix Figure 2. Consequently, it is not surprising that different scoring models tended to "agree" more on the scores for consumers below the median. It is easier to statistically distinguish a consumer that poses, e.g., a 20% default risk from a consumer that poses a 10% default risk than it is to distinguish a consumer that poses a 2% default risk from a consumer that poses a 1% default risk.

2.2.4   Magnitude of Differences across Scoring Models

The correlation and the scatter-plots show that scores were generally similar across scoring models. What they do not make clear is how many consumers had very similar scores across the different models and how many had large differences in their scores. To evaluate this, consumers were divided up into score categories, and then the categories that consumers fall into using the different scoring models were compared. The categories used are "deciles," groups of 10% of the sample.[14] For example, consumers with VantageScores in the bottom 10% of scores, consumers with scores between the 10th percentile of scores and the 20th percentile of scores, etc.

Figure 5 shows the results of comparing score deciles across scoring models. Note that cells with entries of "0%" have some consumers in them but so few that they round to zero, while blank cells have no consumers.

FIGURE 5: DECILE COMPARISONS

Educational vs. FICO	Rank for FICO Score										
Rank for Educational Score	<10%	<20%	<30%	<40%	<50%	<60%	<70%	<80%	<90%	<100%	All
<100%			0%	0%	0%	0%	1%	2%	3%	4%	10%
<90%		0%	0%	0%	0%	0%	1%	2%	3%	3%	11%
<80%		0%	0%	0%	0%	1%	2%	3%	3%	2%	10%
<70%		0%	0%	0%	1%	2%	3%	3%	1%	0%	10%
<60%	0%	0%	0%	1%	2%	4%	2%	1%	0%	0%	10%
<50%	0%	0%	1%	3%	4%	2%	0%	0%	0%	0%	10%
<40%	0%	1%	2%	5%	2%	0%	0%	0%	0%		10%
<30%	1%	3%	4%	2%	0%	0%	0%				9%
<20%	2%	5%	2%	0%	0%	0%					10%
<10%	7%	2%	0%	0%							10%
All	10%	10%	10%	10%	10%	9%	9%	10%	11%	10%	100%

VantageScore vs. Educational	Rank for Educational Score										
Rank for VantageScore	<10%	<20%	<30%	<40%	<50%	<60%	<70%	<80%	<90%	<100%	All
<100%			0%	0%	0%	0%	0%	1%	3%	5%	10%
<90%			0%	0%	0%	0%	1%	2%	4%	3%	10%
<80%		0%	0%	0%	0%	1%	2%	3%	3%	1%	10%
<70%			0%	0%	1%	2%	4%	2%	1%	0%	10%
<60%		0%	0%	1%	2%	3%	2%	1%	1%	0%	10%
<50%	0%	0%	1%	2%	4%	2%	1%	0%	0%	0%	10%
<40%	0%	1%	2%	4%	3%	1%	0%	0%	0%		10%
<30%	1%	2%	4%	2%	0%	0%	0%	0%			10%
<20%	3%	4%	2%	1%	0%	0%	0%				10%
<10%	6%	3%	1%	0%	0%						10%
All	10%	10%	10%	10%	10%	10%	10%	10%	10%	10%	100%

VantageScore vs. FICO	Rank for FICO Score										
Rank for VantageScore	<10%	<20%	<30%	<40%	<50%	<60%	<70%	<80%	<90%	<100%	All
<100%		0%	0%	0%	0%	0%	1%	2%	3%	3%	10%
<90%			0%	0%	0%	1%	1%	2%	3%	4%	10%
<80%		0%		0%	1%	1%	1%	3%	3%	2%	10%
<70%	0%	0%	0%	0%	1%	2%	3%	2%	1%	1%	10%
<60%	0%	0%	0%	1%	2%	3%	3%	1%	0%	0%	10%
<50%	0%	0%	1%	3%	3%	2%	1%	0%	0%	0%	10%
<40%	0%	1%	2%	4%	2%	1%	0%	0%	0%	0%	10%
<30%	1%	3%	3%	2%	0%	0%	0%	0%		0%	10%
<20%	3%	3%	2%	0%	0%	0%	0%	0%			9%
<10%	6%	3%	1%	0%	0%						10%
All	10%	10%	10%	10%	10%	9%	9%	10%	11%	10%	100%

Figure 6 summarizes the results presented in Figure 5. It shows that most consumers, 78 - 86% depending on the comparison, had scores that were in the same decile or in adjacent deciles for each of the two scoring models. A sizeable minority, however, 11 - 16%, had scores that were two deciles away from each other across the scoring models, and a small number, 3 - 6%, have scores that were three or more deciles away from each other.

FIGURE 6: DECILE ANALYSIS

Educational vs. FICO		Cumulative
Decile match (green)	42% (75,592)	42% (75,592)
Adjacent deciles (light green)	43% (76,813)	85% (152,405)
Two deciles off (yellow)	11% (20,436)	97% (172,841)
Three or more deciles off (red)	3% (5,736)	100% (178,577)
Total	100% (178,577)	100% (178,577)

FICO vs. Vantage		Cumulative
Decile match (green)	34% (60,596)	34% (60,596)
Adjacent deciles (light green)	44% (78,388)	78% (138,984)
Two deciles off (yellow)	16% (28,007)	94% (166,991)
Three or more deciles off (red)	6% (10,718)	100% (177,709)
Total	100% (177,709)	100% (177,709)

Educational vs. Vantage		Cumulative
Decile match (green)	42% (76,435)	42% (76,435)
Adjacent deciles (light green)	44% (81,275)	86% (157,710)
Two deciles off (yellow)	11% (20,472)	97% (178,182)
Three or more deciles off (red)	3% (5,669)	100% (183,851)
Total	100% (183,851)	100% (183,851)

2.2.5 Economically Meaningful Differences across Scoring Models

The decile comparisons show how many consumers had scores from different models that were in substantially different portions of the score distribution. These differences, however, did not necessarily translate into meaningful differences between outcomes consumers might expect, based on the scores they obtain, and actual outcomes, based on the scores that creditors actually use to evaluate them. In order to evaluate this it was necessary to identify differences between scores that would be meaningful in the marketplace. Creditors often use scores by establishing score ranges and treating consumers within a range the same for purposes of underwriting or pricing. The use of scores and score categories varies across product markets, and within product markets different creditors use scores differently. In order to evaluate how often meaningful differences would occur we divided score distributions into a set of ranges. These ranges reflect an approximation of how scores are used; this does not reflect the use of scores in any one market or by any one creditor. Consumers were categorized into different score bins for FICO scores and educational scores:

- Below 620;
- Between 620 and 680;
- Between 680 and 740; and
- Above 740.

For VantageScores, consumers were categorized by taking the percentiles associated with each of the FICO score thresholds and applying that percentile cut-point to the distributions of VantageScores. For example, a 620 FICO score is the 25th percentile of the FICO score distribution, so the lowest score category of VantageScores was made up of scores below the 25th percentile of the VantageScore distribution. Similarly, a FICO score of 680 represents the 38th percentile of scores, so the next lowest range of VantageScores was the 25th to 38th percentiles.

Figure 7 shows these comparisons for each of the pairs of scores rounded to the nearest whole percent:

FIGURE 7: SCORE RANGE COMPARISONS

Educational vs. FICO	FICO Score				
Educational Score	< 620	620 - 680	680 - 740	> 740	All
>740	0%	0%	4%	39%	44%
680 – 740	0%	3%	9%	3%	15%
620 – 680	3%	9%	3%	0%	15%
< 620	23%	3%	0%	0%	26%
All	27%	15%	16%	42%	100%

Educational vs. VantageScore	Educational Score				
Rank for VantageScore	< 620	620 - 680	680 - 740	> 740	All
Over 55%	0%	0%	5%	40%	45%
< 55%	1%	5%	8%	3%	17%
< 38%	4%	7%	2%	0%	13%
< 25%	22%	3%	0%	0%	25%
All	27%	15%	16%	43%	100%

FICO vs. VantageScore	FICO Score				
Rank for VantageScore	< 620	620 - 680	680 - 740	> 740	All
Over 55%	0%	1%	7%	39%	47%
< 55%	1%	5%	7%	4%	17%
< 38%	4%	6%	2%	0%	13%
< 25%	21%	2%	0%	0%	24%
All	27%	15%	16%	43%	100%

Figure 8 summarizes the results from the above figures. It shows that most consumers, 73 – 80%, were in the same score categories across the different scoring models. This means that the scores consumers receive will usually give them an accurate understanding of how creditors, using another scoring model, would perceive them. Most of the remaining consumers, 19 – 24%, would likely have a moderate but meaningfully different impression of their credit score than would a creditor using the other score. A very small portion, 1 – 3%, would receive a very different impression than would a creditor using the other score. These findings rely on consumers being sophisticated enough to know how a score they receive might translate into broad pricing or underwriting categories used in the marketplace and in the particular score ranges used here. If some creditors use narrower score ranges, then a smaller share of consumers going to those creditors would have an accurate view.

FIGURE 8: SCORE RANGE ANALYSIS

FICO vs. Educational		Cumulative
Same score category (green)	80% (142,493)	80% (142,493)
Score category off by 1 (yellow)	19% (34,631)	99% (177,124)
Score category off by 2 or more (red)	1% (1,454)	100% (178,578)
Total	100% (178,578)	100% (178,578)

Educational vs. Vantage		Cumulative
Same score category (green)	77% (141,916)	77% (141,916)
Score category off by 1 (yellow)	22% (39,763)	99% (181,679)
Score category off by 2 or more (red)	1% (2,172)	100% (183,851)
Total	100% (183,851)	100% (183,851)

FICO vs. Vantage		Cumulative
Same score category (green)	73% (129,858)	73% (129,858)
Score category off by 1 (yellow)	24% (42,941)	97% (172,799)
Score category off by 2 or more (red)	3% (4,910)	100% (177,709)
Total	100% (177,709)	100% (177,709)

2.2.6 Results for Population Subgroups

The data provided by the CRAs allows some limited analysis of sub-populations of consumers. In particular, the CRAs provided information on age and ZIP code. While ZIP codes are relatively large areas there is still a fair amount of variation across ZIP codes in income and racial and ethnic makeup. ZIP codes were matched to 2000 Census data on income and race and ethnicity.

Figures 9 and 10 show comparisons of median score percentiles and correlations between different scoring models for consumers in different age categories, in ZIP codes with different median income, and ZIP codes with different racial and ethnic make-ups.[15] They show that different groups had very similar median scores across scoring models. For example, younger consumers[16] had lower median scores than older consumers[17], and this finding was consistent across scoring models. The median score for young consumers was very similar across models, between the 31st and 35th percentiles of the overall score distribution. Similarly, consumers who live in lower-income ZIP codes[18] and consumers who live in ZIP codes with high minority populations[19] had relatively low scores, with median scores in the mid-30s of the overall score distribution across scoring models.

These findings with respect to differences in median scores by age, race and ethnicity, and income are consistent with previous analysis by other researchers, including in a detailed study by the Federal Reserve Board in a 2007 report to Congress.[20] We do not address here the underlying causes of these differences nor the implications for different groups of consumer.

FIGURE 9: MEDIAN SCORE COMPARISONS

	Educational Median	FICO Median	Vantage Median	Difference	Educational Median	FICO Median	Vantage Median	Difference
	Younger				**Older**			
Educational vs. FICO	35	35	-	0	74	74	-	0
Educational vs. Vantage	35	-	31	4	74	-	72	2
FICO vs. Vantage	-	35	32	-3	-	74	73	-1
	Customers in LMI Areas				**Customers in Non-LMI Areas**			
Educational vs. FICO	36	34	-	2	54	52	-	2
Educational vs. Vantage	35	-	35	0	53	-	53	0
FICO vs. Vantage	-	34	36	2	-	52	54	2
	Majority Minority Areas				**Low Minority Areas**			
Educational vs. FICO	36	34	-	2	54	52	-	2
Educational vs. Vantage	35	-	35	0	53	-	53	0
FICO vs. Vantage	-	34	37	3	-	53	55	2

Turning to correlations, Figure 10 shows that scores were slightly more correlated for younger consumers and consumers who live in lower-income or high-minority population ZIP codes. This result is consistent with the finding described above that scores were more highly correlated for consumers with lower scores than for consumers with higher scores.

FIGURE 10: MEDIAN SCORE CORRELATIONS

	Younger		Older
Educational vs. FICO	0.92	>	0.90
Educational vs. Vantage	0.91	>	0.90
FICO vs. Vantage	0.89	>	0.85
	Customers in LMI Areas		Customers in Non-LMI Areas
Educational vs. FICO	0.94	>	0.93
Educational vs. Vantage	0.93	~	0.93
FICO vs. Vantage	0.91	>	0.90
	Majority Minority Areas		Low Minority Areas
Educational vs. FICO	0.94	>	0.93
Educational vs. Vantage	0.93	~	0.93
FICO vs. Vantage	0.90	~	0.90

3. Impact and Policy Implications

This study has found that for a majority of consumers the scores produced by different scoring models provide similar information about the relative creditworthiness of the consumers. That is, if a consumer had a good score from one scoring model the consumer likely had a good score on another model. For a substantial minority, however, different scoring models gave meaningfully different results.

The study found that for 73-80% of consumers different scoring models place consumers in the same category of credit quality. Different scoring models place consumers in credit-quality categories that are off by one category 19-24% of the time. And from 1% to 3% of consumers are placed in categories that are two or more categories apart.

These findings suggest that consumers should avoid relying on scores they purchase as the sole basis for assessing their creditworthiness when making important decisions about obtaining credit. No consumer will know in advance whether the score he or she sees will vary significantly from the score a creditor sees. Thus, each consumer should be prepared for the possibility that the score he or she sees is meaningfully different from the score used by a lender.

In evaluating educational credit scores, consumers should also consider the following:

(1) **Many scores exist in the marketplace**: It is unclear the extent to which consumers understand that multiple scores exist in the marketplace. It is likely that many consumers incorrectly believe that the scores they purchase are the same scores used by lenders in evaluating their applications for credit. As described throughout this paper, literally dozens of different credit models are used by lenders. FICO alone has over 49 credit scoring models.[21] Consumers additionally can purchase a range of educational scores or VantageScores.

(2) **Consumers should check their credit reports for accuracy and dispute any errors**: Credit scores are calculated based on information in a consumer's credit file. Regardless of the credit scoring model used, inaccurate adverse information in a consumer's file (e.g. unpaid accounts that are not the consumer's, accounts described as paid late that were paid on time), can hurt that consumer's credit score. Before shopping for major credit items, consumers should review their credit files for inaccuracies. Each of the nationwide CRAs is required by law to provide credit reports for free to consumers once every 12 months upon request. A consumer can obtain these reports at annualcreditreport.com. Consumers can get information on this and the dispute process at ask cfpb.

(3) **Consumers should shop for credit:** Regardless of variations in educational and commercial scores, or even among scoring models used by lenders (which was analyzed in this study in only a very limited and somewhat indirect manner) consumers benefit by shopping for credit. Even if provided the same score, lenders may offer different loan terms because they operate different risk models or face different competitive pressures. Consumers should not rule themselves out of seeking lower priced credit due to assumptions about their credit score.

Some consumers are reluctant to shop for credit out of fear that they will harm their credit score. Many consumers are generally aware that inquiries by creditors can negatively impact their credit score. However, the potentially negative impact of inquiries on credit scores may be overblown. For example, FICO reports that its scoring models treat multiple inquiries made for either a mortgage, auto, or student loan within the same 30 day-window as a single inquiry. Even when credit inquiries are counted separately, as in the case of credit card applications, each additional credit inquiry will take fewer than 5 points off a FICO score.[22] Other scoring models such as Vantage also do not heavily weight inquiries. An inquiry will take 1 to 5 points off a Vantage score.[23]

(4) **Providers of educational scores should ensure that the potential for score differences is clear to consumers:** This study finds that for a substantial minority of consumers, the scores that consumers purchase from the nationwide CRAs depict consumers' creditworthiness differently from the scores sold to creditors. It is likely that, unaided, many consumers will not understand this fact or even understand that the score they have obtained is an educational score and not the score that a lender is likely to rely upon. Consumers obtaining educational scores may be confused about the usefulness of the score being sold if sellers of scores do not make it clear to consumers before the consumer purchases the educational score that it is not the score the lender is likely to use.

Appendix

APPENDIX FIGURE 1: DEFAULT RISK BY FICO SCORE

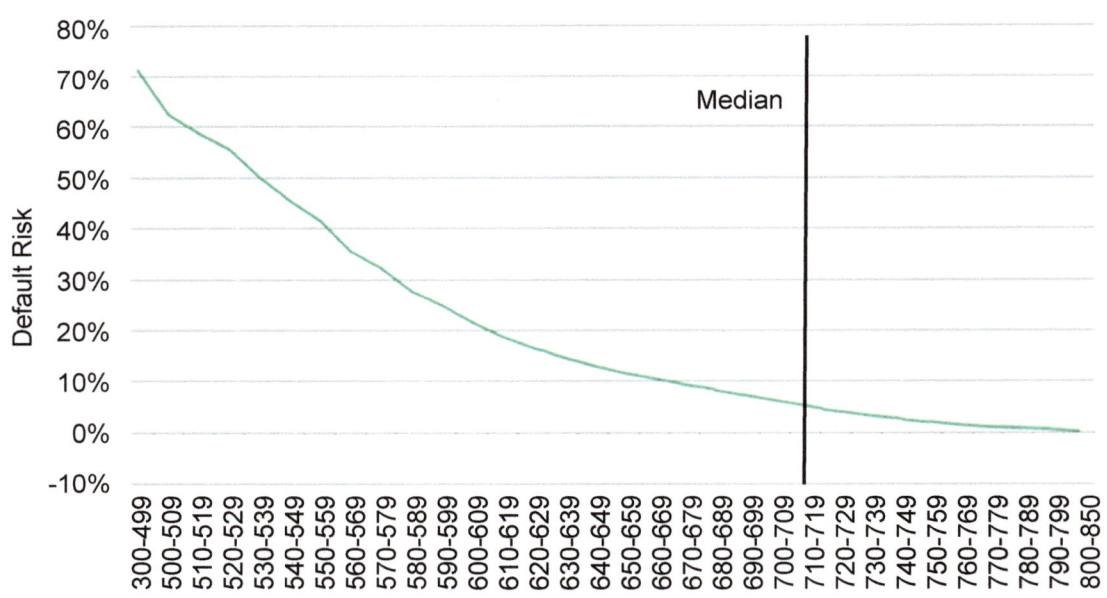

APPENDIX FIGURE 2: 90 DAY DELINQUENCY RATE BY VANTAGESCORE

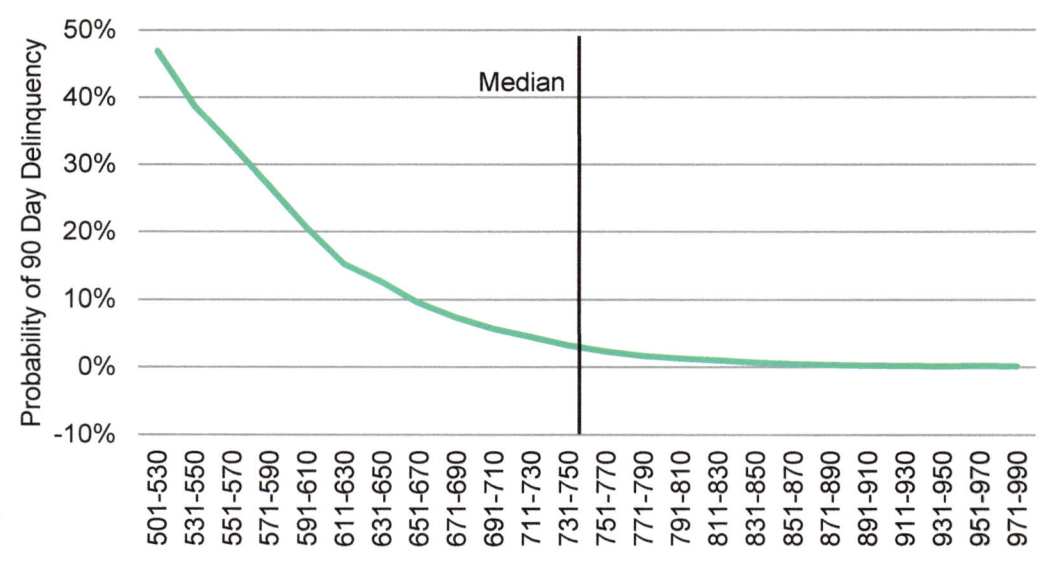

APPENDIX FIGURE 3: SCATTERPLOTS

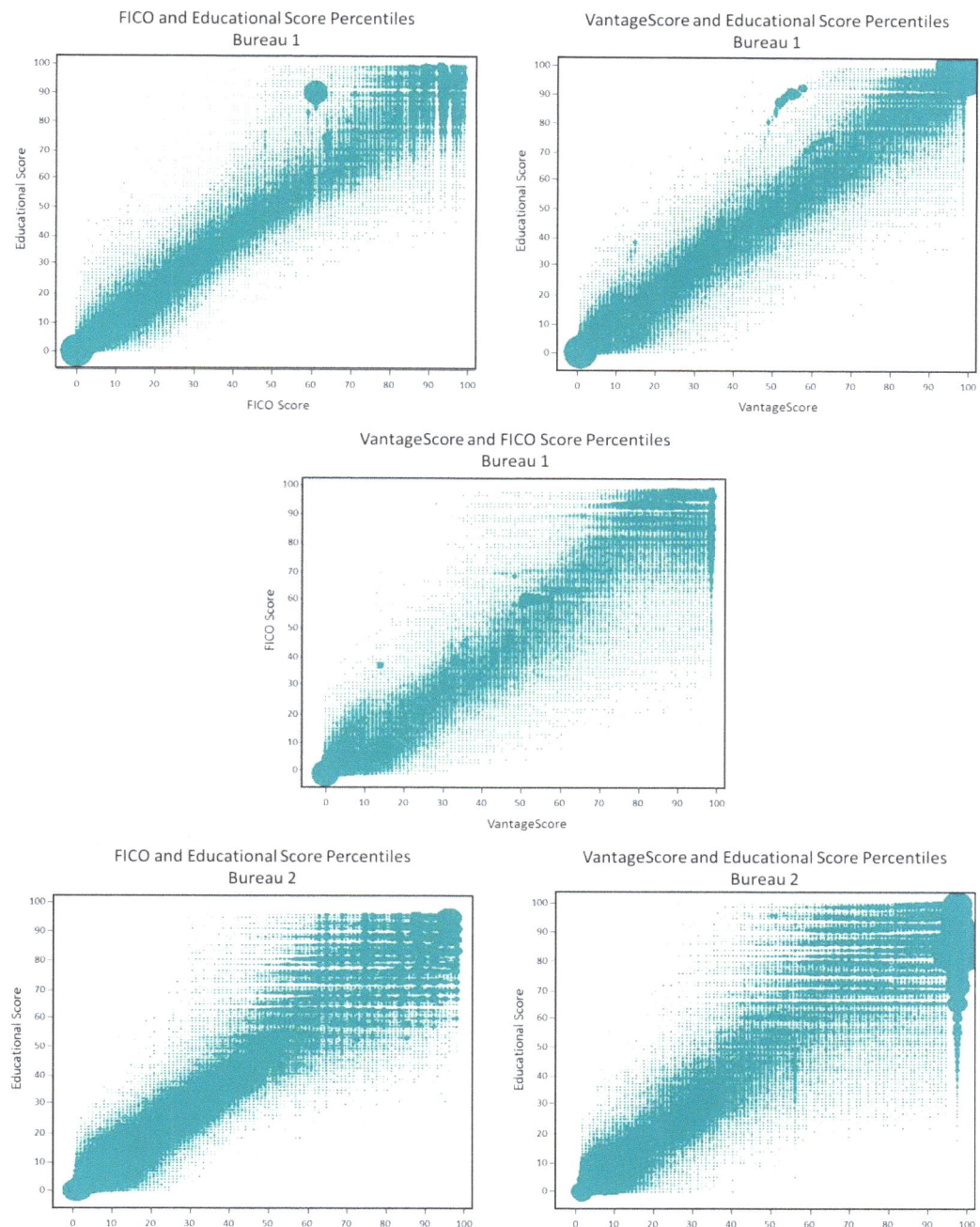

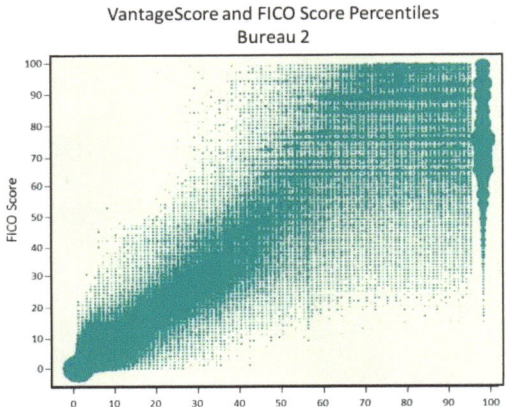

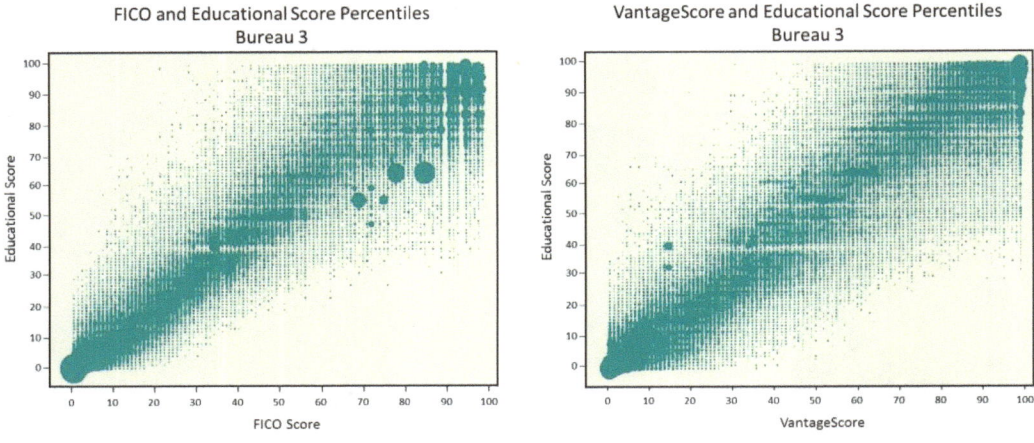

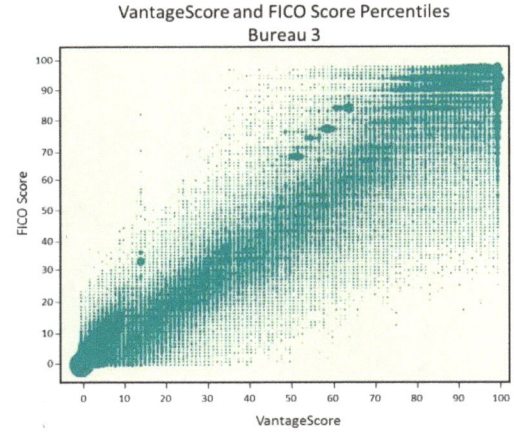

APPENDIX FIGURE 4: SCORE CORRELATIONS

Bureau 1	Overall	Customers Below Median		Customers Above Median
FICO vs. Educational	0.93	0.86	>	0.64
Vantage vs. Educational	0.93	0.82	>	0.68
Vantage vs. FICO	0.90	0.77	>	0.52

Bureau 2	Overall	Customers Below Median		Customers Above Median
FICO vs. Educational	0.90	0.85	>	0.48
Vantage vs. Educational	0.85	0.77	>	0.23
Vantage vs. FICO	0.83	0.78	>	0.13

Bureau 3	Overall	Customers Below Median		Customers Above Median
FICO vs. Educational	0.92	0.84	>	0.55
Vantage vs. Educational	0.91	0.75	>	0.57
Vantage vs. FICO	0.90	0.77	>	0.49

Educational vs. FICO Bureau 1

Rank for Educational Score	<10%	<20%	<30%	<40%	<50%	<60%	<70%	<80%	<90%	<100%	All
<100%			0%	0%	0%	0%	1%	2%	3%	4%	10%
<90%		0%	0%	0%	0%	0%	1%	2%	3%	3%	11%
<80%		0%	0%	0%	0%	1%	2%	3%	3%	2%	10%
<70%		0%	0%	0%	1%	2%	3%	3%	1%	0%	10%
<60%	0%	0%	0%	1%	2%	4%	2%	1%	0%	0%	10%
<50%	0%	0%	1%	3%	4%	2%	0%	0%	0%	0%	10%
<40%	0%	1%	2%	5%	2%	0%	0%	0%	0%		10%
<30%	1%	3%	4%	2%	0%	0%	0%				9%
<20%	2%	5%	2%	0%	0%	0%					10%
<10%	7%	2%	0%	0%							10%
All	10%	10%	10%	10%	10%	9%	9%	10%	11%	10%	100%

Educational vs. FICO Bureau 2

Rank for Educational Score	<10%	<20%	<30%	<40%	<50%	<60%	<70%	<80%	<90%	<100%	All
<100%			0%	0%	0%	0%	1%	2%	3%	4%	11%
<90%			0%	0%	0%	1%	2%	2%	2%	2%	9%
<80%			0%	0%	0%	1%	2%	2%	2%	2%	10%
<70%		0%	0%	0%	1%	2%	3%	2%	2%	1%	11%
<60%		0%	0%	1%	2%	3%	2%	1%	1%	0%	10%
<50%	0%	0%	0%	2%	4%	2%	1%	0%	0%	0%	10%
<40%	0%	1%	3%	4%	2%	0%	0%	0%	0%	0%	10%
<30%	1%	2%	4%	2%	0%	0%	0%	0%			10%
<20%	3%	4%	2%	0%	0%	0%					9%
<10%	6%	3%	0%	0%							10%
All	10%	10%	10%	10%	10%	10%	10%	10%	10%	10%	100%

Educational vs. FICO Bureau 3

Rank for Educational Score	<10%	<20%	<30%	<40%	<50%	<60%	<70%	<80%	<90%	<100%	All
<100%			0%	0%	0%	0%	1%	2%	3%	4%	11%
<90%			0%	0%	0%	1%	2%	3%	3%	3%	12%
<80%		0%		0%	1%	2%	2%	2%	2%	2%	11%
<70%	0%	0%	0%	0%	1%	3%	2%	2%	1%	0%	10%
<60%	0%	0%	0%	1%	3%	3%	1%	1%	0%	0%	9%
<50%	0%	0%	1%	3%	3%	1%	0%	0%	0%	0%	9%
<40%	0%	1%	2%	4%	2%	0%	0%	0%	0%	0%	9%
<30%	1%	2%	4%	2%	0%	0%	0%	0%			10%
<20%	3%	4%	2%	0%	0%	0%					9%
<10%	7%	3%	0%	0%							10%
All	10%	10%	10%	10%	10%	10%	10%	10%	10%	10%	100%

VantageScore vs. Educational Bureau 1

Rank for VantageScore	Rank for Educational Score										
	<10%	<20%	<30%	<40%	<50%	<60%	<70%	<80%	<90%	<100%	All
<100%			0%	0%	0%	0%	0%	1%	3%	5%	10%
<90%			0%	0%	0%	0%	1%	2%	4%	3%	10%
<80%		0%	0%	0%	0%	1%	2%	3%	3%	1%	10%
<70%			0%	0%	1%	2%	4%	2%	1%	0%	10%
<60%		0%	0%	1%	2%	3%	2%	1%	1%	0%	10%
<50%	0%	0%	1%	2%	4%	2%	1%	0%	0%	0%	10%
<40%	0%	1%	2%	4%	3%	1%	0%	0%	0%		10%
<30%	1%	2%	4%	2%	0%	0%	0%	0%			10%
<20%	3%	4%	2%	1%	0%	0%	0%				10%
<10%	6%	3%	1%	0%	0%						10%
All	10%	10%	10%	10%	10%	10%	10%	10%	10%	10%	100%

VantageScore vs. Educational Bureau 2

Rank for VantageScore	Rank for Educational Score										
	<10%	<20%	<30%	<40%	<50%	<60%	<70%	<80%	<90%	<100%	All
<100%		0%	0%	0%	1%	1%	1%	2%	2%	3%	10%
<90%			0%	0%	0%	1%	2%	2%	2%	3%	10%
<80%			0%	0%	1%	1%	2%	2%	2%	2%	10%
<70%		0%	0%	0%	1%	2%	2%	2%	1%	2%	10%
<60%	0%	0%	0%	1%	2%	2%	2%	1%	1%	1%	10%
<50%	0%	0%	1%	2%	3%	2%	1%	1%	0%	0%	10%
<40%	0%	1%	2%	3%	2%	1%	0%	0%	0%	0%	10%
<30%	1%	2%	4%	2%	1%	0%	0%	0%	0%	0%	10%
<20%	3%	4%	2%	1%	0%	0%	0%				10%
<10%	7%	3%	1%	0%	0%	0%					10%
All	10%	10%	10%	10%	10%	10%	11%	10%	9%	11%	100%

VantageScore vs. Educational Bureau 3

Rank for VantageScore	Rank for Educational Score										
	<10%	<20%	<30%	<40%	<50%	<60%	<70%	<80%	<90%	<100%	All
<100%			0%	0%	0%	0%	1%	2%	3%	4%	10%
<90%			0%	0%	0%	1%	2%	3%	3%		10%
<80%			0%	0%	0%	1%	2%	3%	3%	1%	10%
<70%		0%	0%	0%	1%	1%	3%	3%	2%	1%	10%
<60%	0%	0%	0%	1%	2%	3%	3%	1%	1%	0%	10%
<50%	0%	0%	1%	2%	3%	2%	1%	0%	0%	0%	10%
<40%	0%	1%	2%	3%	2%	1%	0%	0%	0%		10%
<30%	1%	3%	4%	2%	1%	0%	0%	0%			10%
<20%	3%	4%	2%	1%	0%	0%	0%			0%	10%
<10%	7%	3%	1%	0%	0%	0%	0%				10%
All	10%	10%	10%	9%	9%	9%	10%	11%	11%	10%	100%

VantageScore vs. FICO Bureau 1

Rank for VantageScore	Rank for FICO Score										All
	<10%	<20%	<30%	<40%	<50%	<60%	<70%	<80%	<90%	<100%	
<100%		0%	0%	0%	0%	0%	1%	2%	3%	3%	10%
<90%			0%	0%	0%	1%	1%	2%	3%	4%	10%
<80%		0%		0%	1%	1%	1%	3%	3%	2%	10%
<70%	0%	0%	0%	0%	1%	2%	3%	2%	1%	1%	10%
<60%	0%	0%	0%	1%	2%	3%	3%	1%	0%	0%	10%
<50%	0%	0%	1%	3%	3%	2%	1%	0%	0%	0%	10%
<40%	0%	1%	2%	4%	2%	1%	0%	0%	0%	0%	10%
<30%	1%	3%	3%	2%	0%	0%	0%	0%		0%	10%
<20%	3%	3%	2%	0%	0%	0%	0%	0%			9%
<10%	6%	3%	1%	0%	0%						10%
All	10%	10%	10%	10%	10%	9%	9%	10%	11%	10%	100%

VantageScore vs. FICO Bureau 2

Rank for VantageScore	Rank for FICO Score										All
	<10%	<20%	<30%	<40%	<50%	<60%	<70%	<80%	<90%	<100%	
<100%		0%	0%	0%	1%	1%	2%	2%	2%	2%	10%
<90%			0%	0%	1%	1%	2%	2%	2%	2%	10%
<80%		0%		0%	1%	1%	2%	2%	2%	3%	10%
<70%		0%	0%	0%	1%	1%	2%	2%	2%	2%	10%
<60%	0%	0%	0%	1%	2%	2%	2%	2%	1%	1%	10%
<50%	0%	0%	1%	2%	3%	2%	1%	1%	0%	0%	10%
<40%	0%	1%	2%	3%	2%	1%	0%	0%	0%	0%	10%
<30%	1%	2%	4%	2%	1%	0%	0%	0%	0	0%	10%
<20%	3%	4%	2%	0%	0%	0%					9%
<10%	7%	3%	0%	0%	0%	0					10%
All	10%	10%	10%	10%	10%	10%	10%	10%	10%	10%	100%

VantageScore vs. FICO Bureau 3

Rank for VantageScore	Rank for FICO Score										All
	<10%	<20%	<30%	<40%	<50%	<60%	<70%	<80%	<90%	<100%	
<100%		0%	0%	0%	0%	0%	1%	2%	3%	4%	11%
<90%			0%	0%	0%	1%	1%	2%	3%	3%	11%
<80%		0%		0%	1%	1%	2%	2%	3%	2%	11%
<70%	0%	0%	0%	0%	1%	2%	3%	2%	1%	1%	11%
<60%	0%	0%	0%	1%	3%	3%	2%	1%	0%	0%	10%
<50%	0%	0%	1%	3%	3%	2%	1%	0%	0%	0%	10%
<40%	0%	1%	3%	3%	2%	1%	0%	0%	0%	0%	9%
<30%	1%	3%	4%	2%	0%	0%	0%	0%			9%
<20%	3%	4%	2%	0%	0%	0%	0%	0%	0		9%
<10%	6%	3%	1%	0%	0%						10%
All	10%	10%	10%	10%	10%	10%	10%	10%	10%	10%	100%

APPENDIX FIGURE 6: DECILE ANALYSIS

Educational vs. FICO Bureau 1		Cumulative
Decile match (green)	42% (75,592)	42% (75,592)
Adjacent deciles (light green)	43% (76,813)	85% (152,405)
Two deciles off (yellow)	11% (20,436)	97% (172,841)
Three or more deciles off (red)	3% (5,736)	100% (178,577)
Total	100% (178,577)	100% (178,577)

Educational vs. Vantage Bureau 1		Cumulative
Decile match (green)	42% (76,435)	42% (76,435)
Adjacent deciles (light green)	44% (81,275)	86% (157,710)
Two deciles off (yellow)	11% (20,472)	97% (178,182)
Three or more deciles off (red)	3% (5,669)	100% (183,851)
Total	100% (183,851)	100% (183,851)

FICO vs. Vantage Bureau 1		Cumulative
Decile match (green)	34% (60,596)	34% (60,596)
Adjacent deciles (light green)	44% (78,388)	78% (138,984)
Two deciles off (yellow)	16% (28,007)	94% (166,991)
Three or more deciles off (red)	6% (10,718)	100% (177,709)
Total	100% (177,709)	100% (177,709)

Educational vs. FICO Bureau 2		Cumulative
Decile match (green)	36% (71,108)	36% (71,108)
Adjacent deciles (light green)	42% (83,061)	78% (154,169)
Two deciles off (yellow)	15% (29,397)	94% (183,566)
Three or more deciles off (red)	6% (11,932)	100% (195,498)
Total	100% (195,498)	100% (195,498)

FICO vs. Vantage Bureau 2		Cumulative
Decile match (green)	30% (58,889)	30% (58,889)
Adjacent deciles (light green)	38% (73,181)	68% (132,070)
Two deciles off (yellow)	19% (37,182)	87% (169,252)
Three or more deciles off (red)	13% (25,706)	100% (194,958)
Total	100% (194,958)	100% (194,598)

Educational vs. Vantage Bureau 2		Cumulative
Decile match (green)	31% (62,289)	31% (62,3289)
Adjacent deciles (light green)	39% (77,659)	70% (139,948)
Two deciles off (yellow)	18% (34,678)	88% (174,626)
Three or more deciles off (red)	12% (23,181)	100% (197,807)
Total	100% (197,807)	100% (197,807)

Educational vs. FICO Bureau 3		Cumulative
Decile match (green)	38% (63,327)	38% (63,327)
Adjacent deciles (light green)	42% (70,340)	80% (133,667)
Two deciles off (yellow)	15% (24,413)	95% (158,080)
Three or more deciles off (red)	5% (8,364)	100% (166,444)
Total	100% (166,444)	100% (166,444)

Educational vs. Vantage Bureau 3		Cumulative
Decile match (green)	36% (62,314)	36% (62,314)
Adjacent deciles (light green)	43% (74,612)	78% (136,926)
Two deciles off (yellow)	16% (28,314)	94% (163,240)
Three or more deciles off (red)	6% (10,180)	100% (175,420)
Total	100% (175,420)	100% (175,420)

FICO vs. Vantage Bureau 3		Cumulative
Decile match (green)	35% (57,252)	35% (57,252)
Adjacent deciles (light green)	42% (69,584)	77% (126,836)
Two deciles off (yellow)	17% (27,863)	93% (154,699)
Three or more deciles off (red)	7% (10,778)	100% (165,477)
Total	100% (165,477)	100% (165,477)

APPENDIX FIGURE 7: SCORE RANGE COMPARISONS

Educational vs. FICO Bureau 1	FICO Score				
Educational Score	< 620	620 - 680	680 - 740	> 740	All
>740	0%	0%	4%	39%	44%
680 - 740	0%	3%	9%	3%	15%
620 - 680	3%	9%	3%	0%	15%
< 620	23%	3%	0%	0%	26%
All	27%	15%	16%	42%	100%

Educational vs. VantageScore Bureau 1	Educational Score				
Rank for VantageScore	< 620	620 - 680	680 - 740	> 740	All
Over 55%	0%	0%	5%	40%	45%
< 55%	1%	5%	8%	3%	17%
< 38%	4%	7%	2%	0%	13%
< 25%	22%	3%	0%	0%	25%
All	27%	15%	16%	43%	100%

FICO vs. VantageScore Bureau 1	FICO Score				
Rank for VantageScore	< 620	620 - 680	680 - 740	> 740	All
Over 55%	0%	1%	7%	39%	47%
< 55%	1%	5%	7%	4%	17%
< 38%	4%	6%	2%	0%	13%
< 25%	21%	2%	0%	0%	24%
All	27%	15%	16%	43%	100%

Educational vs. FICO Bureau 2	FICO Score				
Educational Score	< 620	620 - 680	680 - 740	> 740	All
>740	0%	0%	5%	51%	56%
680 - 740	0%	3%	9%	3%	16%
620 - 680	3%	5%	2%	0%	10%
< 620	15%	3%	0%	0%	18%
All	18%	12%	16%	54%	100%

Educational vs. VantageScore Bureau 2	Educational Score				
Rank for VantageScore	< 620	620 - 680	680 - 740	> 740	All
Over 55%	0%	0%	3%	42%	45%
< 55%	0%	1%	5%	11%	17%
< 38%	1%	4%	6%	2%	13%
< 25%	17%	5%	2%	0%	25%
All	19%	11%	16%	56%	100%

FICO vs. VantageScore Bureau 2	FICO Score				
Rank for VantageScore	< 620	620 - 680	680 - 740	> 740	All
Over 55%	0%	0%	3%	42%	46%
< 55%	0%	1%	5%	10%	17%
< 38%	1%	4%	6%	2%	13%
< 25%	16%	6%	2%	0%	24%
All	18%	12%	16%	54%	100%

Educational vs. FICO Bureau 3	FICO Score				
Educational Score	< 620	620 - 680	680 - 740	> 740	All
>740	0%	0%	3%	35%	38%
680 - 740	0%	3%	10%	8%	22%
620 - 680	3%	8%	3%	0%	15%
< 620	23%	3%	0%	0%	26%
All	26%	14%	17%	46%	100%

Educational vs. VantageScore Bureau 3	Educational Score				
Rank for VantageScore	< 620	620 - 680	680 - 740	> 740	All
Over 55%	0%	1%	10%	34%	45%
< 55%	1%	5%	9%	2%	17%
< 38%	4%	6%	3%	0%	13%
< 25%	22%	3%	0%	0%	25%
All	27%	15%	22%	36%	100%

FICO vs. VantageScore Bureau 3	FICO Score				
Rank for VantageScore	< 620	620 - 680	680 - 740	> 740	All
Over 55%	0%	1%	7%	40%	48%
< 55%	1%	5%	7%	4%	17%
< 38%	4%	6%	2%	0%	12%
< 25%	21%	2%	0%	0%	23%
All	27%	14%	17%	47%	100%

FICO vs. Educational Bureau 1		Cumulative
Same score category (green)	80% (142,493)	80% (142,493)
One category off (yellow)	19% (34,631)	99% (177,124)
More than one category off (red)	1% (1,454)	100% (178,578)
Total	100% (178,578)	100% (178,578)

Educational vs. Vantage Bureau 1		Cumulative
Same score category (green)	77% (141,916)	77% (141,916)
One category off (yellow)	22% (39,763)	99% (181,679)
More than one category off (red)	1% (2,172)	100% (183,851)
Total	100% (183,851)	100% (183,851)

FICO vs. Vantage Bureau 1		Cumulative
Same score category (green)	73% (129,858)	73% (129,858)
One category off (yellow)	24% (42,941)	97% (172,799)
More than one category off (red)	3% (4,910)	100% (177,709)
Total	100% (177,709)	100% (177,709)

FICO vs. Educational Bureau 2		Cumulative
Same score category (green)	80% (155,618)	80% (155,618)
One category off (yellow)	20% (38,388)	99% (194,006)
More than one category off (red)	1% (1,492)	100% (195,498)
Total	100% (195,498)	100% (195,498)

Educational vs. Vantage Bureau 2		Cumulative
Same score category (green)	68% (135,421)	68% (135,421)
One category off (yellow)	27% (52,707)	95% (188,128)
More than one category off (red)	5% (9,679)	100% (197,807)
Total	100% (197,807)	100% (197,807)

FICO vs. Vantage Bureau 2		Cumulative
Same score category (green)	68% (86,706)	68% (86,706)
One category off (yellow)	28% (54,126)	96% (140,832)
More than one category off (red)	4% (7,949)	100% (194,958)
Total	100% (194,958)	100% (194,958)

FICO vs. Educational Bureau 3		Cumulative
Same score category (green)	75% (125,636)	75% (125,636)
One category off (yellow)	23% (38,961)	98% (164,597)
More than one category off (red)	1% (1,847)	100% (166,444)
Total	100% (166,444)	100% (166,444)

Educational vs. Vantage Bureau 3		Cumulative
Same score category (green)	71% (124,430)	71% (124,430)
One category off (yellow)	26% (46,433)	97% (170,863)
More than one category off (red)	3% (4,557)	100% (175,420)
Total	100% (175,420)	100% (175,420)

FICO vs. Vantage Bureau 3		Cumulative
Same score category (green)	74% (121,776)	74% (121,776)
One category off (yellow)	24% (39,308)	97% (161,084)
More than one category off (red)	3% (4,393)	100% (165,477)
Total	100% (165,477)	100% (165,477)

APPENDIX FIGURE 9: MEDIAN SCORE COMPARISONS

Bureau 1	Educational Median	FICO Median	Vantage Median	Difference	Educational Median	FICO Median	Vantage Median	Difference
	Younger				**Older**			
Educational vs. FICO	35	35	-	0	74	74	-	0
Educational vs. Vantage	35	-	31	4	74	-	72	2
FICO vs. Vantage	-	35	32	-3	-	74	73	-1
	Customers in LMI Areas				**Customers in Non-LMI Areas**			
Educational vs. FICO	36	34	-	2	54	52	-	2
Educational vs. Vantage	35	-	35	0	53	-	53	0
FICO vs. Vantage	-	34	36	2	-	52	54	2
	Majority Minority Areas				**Low Minority Areas**			
Educational vs. FICO	36	34	-	2	54	52	-	2
Educational vs. Vantage	35	-	35	0	53	-	53	0
FICO vs. Vantage	-	34	37	3	-	53	55	2

Bureau 2	Educational Median	FICO Median	Vantage Median	Difference	Educational Median	FICO Median	Vantage Median	Difference
	Younger				**Older**			
Educational vs. FICO					64	66	-	-2
Educational vs. Vantage					63	-	61	2
FICO vs. Vantage					-	66	61	-5
	Customers in LMI Areas				**Customers in Non-LMI Areas**			
Educational vs. FICO	37	36	-	1	52	51	-	1
Educational vs. Vantage	36	-	36	0	52	-	52	0
FICO vs. Vantage	-	37	37	0	-	52	52	0
	Majority Minority Areas				**Low Minority Areas**			
Educational vs. FICO	35	34	-	1	53	52	-	1
Educational vs. Vantage	34	-	34	0	53	-	52	1
FICO vs. Vantage	-	34	35	1	-	52	52	0

Bureau 3	Educational Median	FICO Median	Vantage Median	Difference	Educational Median	FICO Median	Vantage Median	Difference
	Younger				Older			
Educational vs. FICO	35	34	-	1	74	74	-	0
Educational vs. Vantage	35	-	31	4	73	-	70	3
FICO vs. Vantage	-	34	32	-2	-	74	71	-3
	Customers in LMI Areas				Customers in Non-LMI Areas			
Educational vs. FICO	36	34	-	2	56	52	-	4
Educational vs. Vantage	34	-	34	0	55	-	53	2
FICO vs. Vantage	-	34	37	3	-	52	55	3
	Majority Minority Areas				Low Minority Areas			
Educational vs. FICO	36	34	-	2	57	52	-	5
Educational vs. Vantage	34	-	34	0	55	-	53	2
FICO vs. Vantage	-	34	37	3	-	52	56	4

APPENDIX FIGURE 10: MEDIAN SCORE CORRELATIONS

Bureau 1	Younger		Older
Educational vs. FICO	0.92	>	0.90
Educational vs. Vantage	0.91	>	0.90
FICO vs. Vantage	0.89	>	0.85
	Customers in LMI Areas		Customers in Non-LMI Areas
Educational vs. FICO	0.94	>	0.93
Educational vs. Vantage	0.93	~	0.93
FICO vs. Vantage	0.91	>	0.90
	Majority Minority Areas		Low Minority Areas
Educational vs. FICO	0.94	>	0.93
Educational vs. Vantage	0.93	~	0.93
FICO vs. Vantage	0.90	~	0.90

Bureau 2	Younger		Older
Educational vs. FICO			0.88
Educational vs. Vantage			0.80
FICO vs. Vantage			0.78
	Customers in LMI Areas		Customers in Non-LMI Areas
Educational vs. FICO	0.92	>	0.90
Educational vs. Vantage	0.93	~	0.93
FICO vs. Vantage	0.87	>	0.83
	Majority Minority Areas		Low Minority Areas
Educational vs. FICO	0.92	<	0.93
Educational vs. Vantage	0.93	>	0.90
FICO vs. Vantage	0.86	>	0.83

Bureau 3	Younger		Older
Educational vs. FICO	0.90	>	0.87
Educational vs. Vantage	0.87	~	0.87
FICO vs. Vantage	0.89	>	0.84
	Customers in LMI Areas		Customers in Non-LMI Areas
Educational vs. FICO	0.93	>	0.91
Educational vs. Vantage	0.91	>	0.90
FICO vs. Vantage	0.91	>	0.89
	Majority Minority Areas		Low Minority Areas
Educational vs. FICO	0.92	>	0.91
Educational vs. Vantage	0.91	>	0.90
FICO vs. Vantage	0.90	>	0.89

[1] Dodd-Frank Wall Street Reform and Consumer Protection Act, Pub. L. 111-203, sec. 1078, 124 Stat. 1376, 2076 (enacted July 21, 2010).

[2] Consumer Financial Protection Bureau, "The Impact of Differences between Consumer and Creditor-Purchased Credit Scores," (July 19, 2012).

[3] See, e.g., Equifax, Things You Should Know... (online at https://help.equifax.com/app/answers/detail/a_id/386/~/things-you-should-know...) ("The Equifax Credit Score ... is intended for your own educational use. There are numerous credit scores and models available in the marketplace and lenders may use a different score when evaluating your creditworthiness."); Experian, online at www.experian.com ("Experian Credit Score indicates your relative credit risk level for educational purposes and is not the score used by lenders.")

[4] See Equifax product information online, at: https://help.equifax.com/app/answers/detail/a_id/386/~/things-you-should-know...

[5] Experian, FAQ: What is a PLUS Score (online at http://www.nationalscore.com/FAQ.aspx).

[6] CreditKarma, online at http://www.creditkarma.com/preview/score/. This score, unlike the others, is specifically designed to predict risk on new accounts, rather than new and existing accounts.

[7] A lender must provide consumers a credit score if (1) the lender provided credit on material terms that are materially less favorable than the most favorable material terms available to a substantial proportion of consumers from or through that lender based in whole or in part on a consumer report, (2) the consumer applies for a mortgage loan and the mortgage lender uses credit scores, or (3) when the lender takes adverse action against the consumer based in whole or in part on information in a consumer report. See Consumer Financial Protection Bureau, "The Impact of Differences between Consumer and Creditor- Purchased Credit Scores," at 12 (July 19, 2011).

[8] Fannie Mae Selling Guide Announcement 09-29, September 22, 2009, page 2.

[9] The Bureau received only the information described in the body of the report. The Bureau did not receive name, Social Security Number, address information beyond ZIP code, or other identifying information.

[10] Credit scores sold to predict payment behavior for a wide range of products are typically called "generic" scores. When scores are designed more specifically to predict behavior for one type of credit, such as automobile loans or credit cards, they are referred to as "industry" scores. The most specific scores, typically used by individual lenders and calculated from a combination of bureau and other information, are called "custom" scores.

[11] FICO Auto scores had a correlation of 0.99, 0.95, and 0.98 for bureaus 1, 2 and 3 respectively with a generic FICO score. FICO Bank Card scores had a correlation of 0.99, 0.99, and 0.99 for bureaus 1, 2, and 3 respectively with generic FICO scores.

[12] Because older consumers tend to have higher credit scores, the median credit score for this CRA is higher than that of the other two CRAs. Because the correlations across scoring models are lower for consumers with higher credit scores the correlations across scores are lower at this CRA. The results are fully consistent with the different age distribution in this CRA's sample, and therefore we do not believe there are substantial differences in the correlations across models at this CRA but rather that these differences are the result of the sampling differences.

[13] Default risk derived from report of odds ratio of any 90 day delinquency or any derogatory note in trade lines from FICO Score Trend Validation Chart. Default risk was taken as 1/(1+ odds ratio).

[14] Deciles were defined for each score for all consumers that had that score. Rows and columns of the tables do not always add up to exactly 10% because of missing scores. Some consumers in the sample were missing one or more scores, and in each pairwise comparison of the scores the distribution of missing values was not even across all deciles; some deciles had slightly more or slightly less than 10% when missing scores were removed from the table. For example at one bureau, VantageScore was missing on 0.81% of the sample when an educational score was reported. Conversely, the educational score was missing on 0.19% of the sample when VantageScore was reported. FICO scores were missing on 3.44% of the sample when the educational score was provided. Conversely, the educational score was missing on 4.46% of the sample when FICO scores were provided. FICO scores were missing on 3.26% of the sample when VantageScore was provided, and VantageScores were missing on 4.90% of the sample when FICO was provided.

[15] Each comparison across scoring models is for consumers with scores from both models, so the sample used varies across comparisons. This approach was used to ensure that differences across scoring models are driven entirely by differences in the models, and not differences in the sample that has each score. This is why the median score for a given group – such as median VantageScore for young consumers – varies across comparisons.

[16] Younger consumers were defined as those with ages from 18 to 25. The three CRAs did not have consumers below age 18.

[17] Older consumers were defined as those age 62 or more.

[18] Zip codes were matched to 2000 Census ZCTA data and classified into low, moderate, middle and upper income areas. Low and moderate income areas have less than 80 percent of median household income.

[19] High minority population was defined as an area with 50% or more minorities.

[20] Report to Congress on Credit Scoring and its Effects on the Availability and Affordability of Credit, Board of Governors of the Federal Reserve System (August 2007).

[21] New York Times, "Why you have 49 different FICO Scores (online at http://bucks.blogs.nytimes.com/2012/08/27/why-you-have-49-different-fico-scores/).

[22] See http://www.myfico.com/crediteducation/creditinquiries.aspx.

[23] CFPB conversation with Barrett Burns, CEO, VantageScore®, August 28, 2012.